NEWER LIES

DATE DUE

ESSENTIAL POETS SERIES 136

Canada Council
for the Arts

Conseil des Arts
du Canada

ONTARIO ARTS COUNCIL
CONSEIL DES ARTS DE L'ONTARIO

Guernica Editions Inc. acknowledges the support of The Canada Council for the Arts.
Guernica Editions Inc. acknowledges the support of the Ontario Arts Council.

DANIEL JALOWICA

NEWER LIES

GUERNICA

TORONTO · BUFFALO · CHICAGO · LANCASTER (U.K.)
2006

Antonio D'Alfonso, editor
Guernica Editions Inc.
P.O. Box 117, Station P, Toronto (ON), Canada M5S 2S6
2250 Military Road, Tonawanda, N.Y. 14150-6000 U.S.A.

Distributors:
University of Toronto Press Distribution,
5201 Dufferin Street, Toronto (ON), Canada M3H 5T8

Gazelle Book Services, White Cross Mills, High Town,
Lancaster LA1 1XS U.K.

Independent Publishers Group,
814 N. Franklin Street, Chicago, Il. 60610 U.S.A.

First edition.
Printed in Canada.

Legal Deposit — First Quarter
National Library of Canada
Library of Congress Catalog Card Number: 2005931738
Library and Archives Canada Cataloguing in Publication
Jalowica, Daniel
Newer lies / Dan Jalowica.
Poems.
ISBN 1-55071-228-4
I. Title.
PS8569.A4256N49 2005   C811'.54   C2005-905218-X

Contents

Time of Day 9
In Harness 10
New Rule 11
Glance Ahead 12
Vacation Pay 13
Newer Lies 14
Party Girl 15
Mask and Storm 16
What I Need from You 17
Wide Lens 18
Cover Story 19
Coming of Age 20
Longer View 21
Narrow Columns 22
War Fever 23
China Hunger 24
Quick Study 25
Prisoner 26
White Road 27
Hunter 28
There to Here 29
Perpetual Notion 30
Red Skies 31
Love Nailed 32
What We Have 33
Slow Mail 34
Lost Keys 35
Deep Wrinkles 36
Old Figure and Ground 37
Monarch 38
Nods Divine 39
Sad Bride 40
North Country 41
Long Haul 42
Brushed Chrome 43
Marathon 44
Plain Spirits 45
Splinters 46

Sleep Lines 47
Storm Door 48
Hands 49
High Life 50
Protective Colours 51
Altitude Losses 52
Farm Journal 53
Till Tomorrow 54
Fast Glimpse 55
Serious Goodbyes 56
Drowning Pond 58
Watchtower 59
Best Instincts 60
Blood Pressure 61
Tour of Duty 62
Quietist Companion 63
Night Ride 64
Rest in Time 65
Turning Home 66
Far Light 67
Harmony and Sea 68
Look North 69

Acknowledgements 70

To Judith, Antonio, and all hungry ghosts

When I think back to my home, where there is no one left now, it always seems to me that things must have been different back then. Then, you knew (or perhaps you sensed it) that you had your death inside you as a fruit has its core.

Rainer Maria Rilke

Time of Day

We know poverty and the mainstay
afternoon with its pillaged harmonies;
dawn dead and night yet to suffer.
We forget nothing. We have our temple
rags, our drifting locutions, our soft
harness of fever. We know flight, war
clouds, and many masters by heart.

In Harness

I do collect clouds on the open and even days –
the black-hearted ones as well as the saints,
tumbling in their thin Eden.
Flash their faces – cards on the table.
Five-card stud – that's the game to play
to get out, to rise, to pin your personality
to higher beings. You want to catch your balance;
place your wheatfields here, your chapel
in the forest there; perhaps a film of dew
to tart up the morning? In fact, lend me
a little light rain, my friend, and a plan
and tell me 'bout tomorrow. I think
I'm ready for another kick, another
trespass against wicked time. My henchmen
say victory draws near. They tense their
fingers and speak of breakthroughs.

I'll remember the dream next time;
my teamed horses under brilliant skies.
I'll shift out of the shadows and stir
my weary lined hope once more.

New Rule

In a room crowded with stainless-steel narratives,
ripe with beings glittering in convergence, our story
machines thrive on proper voltages. Meat hangs
from hooks in cruel Mexican sunshine. Yes,
conversions hit with a painful sting. Heat ripples
on all familiar planets. Or roads cross
at fear and conviction among relaxed animals.
Our spines cramped in viscous media, marrow
in a spill, our lips firm to the touch of words –
and, yes, we are willing to be true.

Glance Ahead

The truth may be a shy river
coursing through your temples.
Heartache in dark collaboration.
I conjure your softened face
and plenitude in loyal sun.
Fight lucid forgeries bedded
in hushed chords. Nurture faint hope
amidst bristling second guesses.

Vacation Pay

Chance wades shallow in some of the sore
corners of winter: More conflagrations to come.
Roar of the masters swollen to maddening repetition.
I barely recall freedom. Here, the bones arranged
in keys. (No majors, no strict lessons.)
Only the dance – floor scarred – beneath hard light
and harder rules. Post-human, past caring.

The fight's a novel. All our animals dead.
Our borrowed faith broadens every day
in tired lines and stranded faces. Blackouts.
Drive deeper still. Listen, you'll hear them weep,
their pain awash in the cramped fields.

Newer Lies

That was life, that brash mazurka
with its hellion fingertips and sloe-gin archipelagos.
This must be living, revised, a hand
gently pressing withered flesh.
Take the two of us – nimble spectres
in a congregation of thundering senses
– take love.
Out there high, descending, ending
with its throat pressed to the blade
of urgent razor revelation. Forgiveness forgotten.
Jammed throttles. A throng of raw hunches.
We may sit graveside, regular in dilemma,
undisturbed by the chill. Or my painting
past. All the aphoristic keys in tune.
A tour of the lulled layers, cradled motion.
A long story and a train ride
couched in stops, stills, cuts.

Party Girl

Long into the drift of highways
find a gift, a small victory spelled out
by a lover lost in naked walls
and lonely with her sirens in bright
painted screams – a nest of puzzles.

She's mastered all the arrangements.
Long after sleep. Marvellous armies
drawn into manoeuvres. It's the old
grapple with bitter ends and delusion;
it's the delicious removal of masks
that create her stock in trade.

Mask and Storm

On time for an appointment behind glass
on the spent side of an emotional fiction
– Cinco de Mayo wafted up from streets
far below – I freshen another set of lies.

Labour silent – riddled with doubt –
beneath a low ceiling. My palms burn
with risks. I can hunger only,
again, for the raw state.

Words build their world from a hidden palate.
Another generation on young legs
sprints across the salt marshes. I move
among faces, the long and short
versions of transport. The face of this day
painted, hung, fractured; the face of a dream
yearning for eyes of its own.

What I Need from You

Eloping from the ruins
of a private lie I waken
dawn from her basalt tomb.
Rouse a dog-and-pony show
to touch a shy mantic
lover in her torn empire.

I need your love. I need
to throw down roads
across these painkilling continents
with their soft illogical music,
their frightened animals,
their moody heartbeat not yet
my own, not yet possessed.

Wide Lens

We never quite intended to spend life
times in the shallows, in the shadow
of weariness, our limbs thrust into hermitage
spaces. Never allowed the birds to sing.
Nor tenderness – its thin hands in sluggish
exploration of the unspoken word – obdurate now,
piled against sleepers and their pain.
So many alibis ripening out there
in the russet earth where I meet you
and your living story lines all taut,
vital, keyed to victory. Perfect.

Cover Story

Summer is a speed, a black expanse
of car and space, reckless for the feel
of it. They've given me keys to the city.
I'm back in the gap. Familiar to plain
sordid and back again. It's all exotic
breezes and low-slung motel splashes.
Glass fragments on the breath. Tourists.
Crackerjack bars in a line along Main.
Military secrets under a shell of night.
I place legends behind a veil. Major
death on the television. No vision at all
when the measureless morning light arrives.
Submarines off shore. Surveillance reaches
into high noon. Thank God they're here
– harpsichords among the palms; silver
in the sand. I burden myself with nerves.
Listen for terse statements from the top.
Fill hungry space with a desperate scheme.
And only laugh when they call my name.

Coming of Age

It was a high step; I sat there
and wept alone in my foreign clothes
at the gates of the saved city.

My hands out of reach, folded
into their own suffering –
no blood, no bold amplitudes.

Only hope in a thin thin
wash against the hides
of shrill nervous beasts.

Longer View

Snow on my pines. Now I know
this day's all magic
as it tries to sneak inside.
I know you love me. But the war
stays close. All the colours
wash away in moonlight. Things
stripped and torn by logic
on every side. I know you
will wait, I know you breathe,
there – just beyond my solo fingertips.

Narrow Columns

We paint the full circle
come by way of contraries
and rough-hewn desires,
study branches leaning
toward motion. Lay claim
to losses and tarry
in our own fulsome cries
ravaged by stimulants.

I call to you to nurture
my fledgling lives
cupped in the cold curves
of the open road.

War Fever

Each day the guardians run out
into the streets of hell. Our lives
will never be the same. That much
certain. The inside story craves
a battlefield. And more
televisions; more penetration
by pictures. We do need
our prisons. And the arousing
friction of weapons. So many
fears. So many budding
pleasures and promises
made inside many operating rooms.
Surgery a success, always, of course.
Mademoiselle flees, a tramp
in her night stockings flying
to some remote heaven.

China Hunger

I am a slight figure from a thin brush
in an icy wind. My eyes filled with tears.
I need your loving face. Your yew trees.

I'm out here among the ghosts now. They touch
down one by one in morose rhythms. Alight
in a blind white ruthless storm of regret.

Quick Study

I navigate the new life
with a slash-and-turn attitude;
lean through sanguinary time,
a lodestone in my pact.

No lean back into sentimental
corners with their black forges
and their manifestos. No more
morning strangers opulent in the dew.

I can only harvest impossible souvenirs
from this private sea, acquire guns,
move intimately among the apparitions
of these brash resilient hours.

Prisoner

Tawdry cast of a new century just
out of sight, I turn to the exact
novelties, trace a superb race
of fears modelled to the nines.

Where are my black fields, their fogs,
intoxicating scents, and crude alchemies?

Here in town they know our numbers,
know our huggermugger act,
our faces by the bloodless pack.

White Road

Behind closed doors you promised me
wisdom but I see only harvests,
candlelight, dry tinder time.

Events fold neatly into themselves;
festival lights recede in parallel
lines grown digital now,
odourless and true.

Thickened skin of a hand reaches
into the dream. Far from dusty fields,
planted feet, and glass cool
against fingers, water against throats;
voices set free in noonday clarity.
That's the system, leading. The rest
is only a cry dying among ruptured buildings.
In their robes the old men speak
in sighed lines, deal from stained hands,
pick with their withered claws
at the wings of creatures adrift
in sticky pools of time.

Hunter

All I have left
to follow: a slattern trail
over rock in wry enduring
hills. Bitter to the caring
soul. Dragging my bone-marrow
emotions in flushed pursuit
of God – gone now, stone cold
in the clutch of flesh.
Black and white
– clipped and eclipsed.
All I have left: memory
and its deliberate burials
– ruined by duration,
torn in the glare of love
and faded devotion.

There to Here

Your eyes fill with tears, clouded skies
and wishes. A run at black-and-white
days. Hardy paired souls, we crave
in clearest voices, duality and dashed hopes;
caresses high in aspiring pines. A bell,
a bird. A vision stroked, a distant rumour
healing. No stronger sun. No longer.

Perpetual Notion

A factory looms at the foot
of the street. Children away.
Hedges, no trees. Your tiny
white house a neat whisky
playground. Spun gold
and sails. You slip time
into your big pockets
with a big smile, no cheap rye
victory this. Lights on,
they burn straight through noon.
Shots sing out, high, I hear a figure
fall, fading through furniture, floors,
the trail suddenly cold. Walls
impenetrable again. Sycophant
organisms on your night table.
Mirrors tense, too. Scents of true
reflection. And saints, and visual aids
and a master. And a journey.
A search winding down with the planet.
A stagger into a clean street
where soft blinding twilight rolls.
No panic in the liquid reach of holy mind.

Red Skies

It's a North End rumbling with its rumours
and spilled aggravations; a tumble, a chill
of wakened spirits. A lace of frost; a hearth.
A burnt cross and widened worlds. Fine life
in a metal flood. Assembly lines; the longitudes
of nightmare. Banquets. Dead drivers. And every
last goddamned corner bleached by corrosive winds.

Love Nailed

I am blind in these narrow rooms;
a slim broken shadow hobbled and foundering;
a full season come round in tart night.

Eye open slowly, to hope and terror;
close with a silver click on tomorrow.
I dream my dime-thin brush with forever
and final counts; the war no longer far.

I build a calming fiction with the tips
of these hungry fingers. Fashion a life
here in the wreckage. Belly exposed,
mind skipping stones across water.

What We Have

You've chased away
the dust
and the books and the flesh
and I've raced to find a code;
discovering nothing but
indecipherable space.

And days and uncurtained nights
rife with right-minded invaders.
The leer of sage rulers attends
us at the grunting wheel.

We have our histories
fenced in their corner.
We have our glory and bloodline ventures,
our blue sons, our rainbow solutions,
and all manner of other flowers dead on arrival.

Slow Mail

I'll be found by a hungry wind
I'll be down in a wrong time gone
wishing at break of broken day.

Your name to be a river; your name
to be a sea of vibrant logic. Rage on.

My field to be blackened unploughed earth.
Too much blood. Too many weathered moons.
All too many ordinary lies to be undone.

Lost Keys

Storm town lives in me
in the speech of typewriters,
in memory. A voice blown
into tree tops alongside
a round sky.
Hear a coo? Lovetalk,
and rasp of uneasy lungs.
Listen to a light song of pen tip
across paper. Distant crumpling of cars.
Formulas for rain. Receptive skin
in play. Bristle of leaves
in their blankets. Factory whistles.
The languid voice of snakes.

Deep Wrinkles

I'll vouch for small harvests
in the fields of silence
before birdsong in darkness
punctuated by tiny old stars.

Our final surrender to power
lends itself to the stretch to grace.
All the rattled soothsayers
with flushed faces say go

on to glory.

Old Figure and Ground

I'm poised here with my pride
and my enslaved cities reddening below.
This time of day I've only martyrs
and mirrors to keep my attention.
I can't put time back, can't put
the right moves at my beck and call.
Let all the worlds bleed their molten
colours; it's only heat and death,
or consummation. If I dream I dream
cool alcohol baths. Veined marble,
and buoyant years. I'll be back,
human again, after all, skin healed
from the horde of pointed questions,
reeling with answers. I have tried
prayer, given my eyes to the light
of stars crusted top dead centre
in blackness. I love only machines
— squat, unpoetic, confident
in their checkerboard squares. Each
move assured. Each breath consolidates
control. The drifters are back,
their eyes blank, their twitching skin
a scandal. All these lower layers of being,
hell, we'll take care of them with a little handiwork
and mettle. We can't have time for these ancient
emotions. Let us show you our triumphs,
our genius, our vigorous toil in new territories.

Monarch

Summer. No music.
No touch-tone friendship.
No storm. Will massed,
knotted. Awareness
a dull extinguished trinket.
Among other losses. Salvation
by lottery. Eternity a rent
in soothing fabric. I reign
faceless in ravaged towns
clawed by definition.
No eyes for the neutral sky,
no globes cupped in driven
space. Only stones and
their turned-in faces
and flaws. And their thirst
for bliss and stolen chances
for a fleeting appearance
in blaring carnival time.

Nods Divine

In frail time in cunning
she closes her omens and lean green eyes.

Her solid colours cross convention.
Her amphibious logic teams
with inviolate edges. She crouches
to invigorate a tabletop landscape.

She hones her names with tender might.

Our ships ease through redemptive shallows.

Sad Bride

Precise worlds open like cheap flowers.
In snow. Against black rocks.
Among small bodies of water.
In grasp of tiny thawed animals.
Machinery of sharpened sense.
A focus and a roam of backroads. Conquest.
Damned past. Only profound buildings
from the ground up. Touchstones abandoned.
A good slash at context. Fear killed.
Uncertainty destroyed. We do
have our vestigial talents. Artefacts
of a strange and brutal history.
We can sort the facts, Ma'am,
chew on results, like a factory.
And welcome alien instruction.

North Country

Yes, you are pure, you are pure
longing disguised, a mastered tribulation.
I've seen you dress blithely
in seconds. Place masks on all
your fated awakenings. Hoard space
and bury time in nine territories.
Hew to finely draughted plans
and their impossible eventualities.
A blue shafted light slants hard.

Long Haul

We have yet our still lives, our faint
metred trespasses fading into distance.
Our basking forms and pyres, waiting
on fire. A fiddle with a glimpse at ease
of graft. One harsh decline.
Time in its yellow rage angled
to our precious upright rotted keepsakes.

Brushed Chrome

Laugh with your furrowed mood in a heaven.
Take your byes and your stricken limbs
in their immense exposure. Leave the moon
to find its way, roll its wide wheel of light
through banks of ragged cloud.

In the streets our children starve.
A world stolen, never to be returned.
You press the answer, only distance
opens in return, outward, upon a structure
moist with hope. Learn every last nuance
of hibernation; master the hypnotic voice
that reaches into every dream. A past
compressed razor thin. A future open
to flashing heights and plain solid landings.

Forge your brittle show
for the artificial season, in refrain.
Plan for peculiar grace
with faintly frosted bouquets.

Marathon

You burn your journals
in an orgy of insight,
I turn to poison spirits
roosting in our monsoon
cerebrations, no thought
of bodies, burdened
by angular souls. We fought
the slide, the turn to graceless
fortune, on its tiny wheels.
Gorged on fabrication.
At terrible holy speeds.

Plain Spirits

No query in the lines
of your face, Darling.
We have spring late in coming,

and your patience, so fluid.
The old faces remain
in every marketplace, they want

to speak. I have no patience.
And very few benevolent passions.

If only our victories weren't always
bruised flowers in tidy arrangement
beneath a dying sun.

Splinters

Carnival over, you're back,
again in the heat of day,
puzzling at such a plain scene,
the one inside with its vital
exchanges with faint strangers.
There's nothing else you can do.
Even here a cold god may strike.
Certainty dies in an instant.
You think you're special. Then
weapons appear; the camps stand
full, sinister, undeniable.
Fear and trained muscle,
and confrontation. Clarity
breaks in, a thief. Mind is victory,
rigged to lose the past.
The breeze has its dreamers.
White ash over red coals.

Sleep Lines

I think her skin I feel her cry
sense. Breath in a flicker, immortal.
I watch her stand stolidly
at frayed edge of recall.
Not calling. Tears in another language;
a spill of fears thawed
from musculature. Lost spouses,
in silent Siberian spring. Borderlines
severe; etch of kerchief, framed
faces burdened by hard versions
of time. The river tiny. Stories untold.

Storm Door

I am behind glass, fields of bleached snow
to each horizon. Hieroglyphs filter
through dreaming fingers. A jab and reel
from one state to another, all naked branches,
disordered minds. A whisper from the old
late hungers. Noisy bones and silent snubs.
Wedding put off, to the rainy season.
Journey smudged, steeled to some uncertain destination.

Hands

Planet motions slow, the wicks
burning low in last dramatic gesture,
we climb into the backroom ruins,
stacked with old tales. Trump cards
married now. Friendship on the half
shell. Short remnants of longing
pasted into wholeness. Teasing dread.
Green fields lost and forgotten.
Remember our blind powers,
our reasons for strength? All those visits
from the quieter gods?
Hell and warm hands. Sullen features
tall in memory. Bodies aligned
precisely with the east.

High Life

Each hometown craves the dry exertions
of reluctant memory. Thrill-seekers swarm
every high-altitude city. Some kind of greasy
exhilaration there, rubbed against clouds,
steeped fog and sterile conquest.

But light's a preserve of the restless
gods, trembling with their best intentions.
Admire the sheen of the ascendant body
in a state of fame. Prepare to travel
farther. A well-machined crew stands by.

Protective Colours

I ask for blue cities, live in clear
apprehension of blackness, imagine
patience on the plains. There. A rainbow
on my street. Finally. The sign. And all
the nerves in a torn creature soothed.
For a moment, a sense of skin
against tomorrow.

Altitude Losses

One war over another begins then fades.
Acuity gone. Mood and detail on the lam.
They're fifties; they're hope in the avenue.
Flay of light against waters still
against steel towers. Tiny red houses
and sidewalks in August glaze.
Wagons and forties pickups in frame of sight.
Body free and feasting upon space,
wrestling with fences, trees,
back porches, restless thoughts –
scent of children, charm of petals fallen
to the pavement. Interiors of little consequence
in big worlds. Backyards, perhaps. Weather,
certainly. No question it's out of the way,
the easy part – photographs disconnected
from memory. Bodies silent in grey variation.

Healing amid the drifts. Ramshackle
happy states of review. Full story unknown
to this day, never to be known
in a wash of beings striking flinty surfaces
of earth and time. Forgiving altered states,
ours, servants of the malleable narrative.

Farm Journal

Soil frozen. Horizon obliterated
by snow; down to the small worlds.
And crowds of round surfaces
on crusade – the slow life leading.
Madness and sinister serenades.
A fast merge in a drowsy century;
eyeless tarantella.

Till Tomorrow

Market day we say vision
– peppers, shrimp,
tomatoes in the mouths
of huge fish.
A crippled drunk
and his lost legs.
The blind on their pilgrimage
in a rippled sea of colours.
Say canvas chairs. Salt. An ocean
only sensed. Birds of prey
in ominous congealed air.
Crashed waves. Minor chords.
Tragic statuary.

Fast Glimpse

Every morning to night river
takes me there to her, composed
now in liquid time passing.
Every drowned flower a mission
in frozen space. All points east,
west – turned to ravenous memory.
Coarse hands fit smoothly
into familiar tools. Unbearable
sadness written in bent bodies.

Serious Goodbyes

Night falls down hard
against me in my mirrored rooms
in my crystal palaces thronged
by memories and old amber lives.

I continue to arrive
in the same older places
changed in shade, in broken rhythms.

Fruit softens on a sill. Will
tightens. I dread the heavy carcass
departure carries. Intention rides
a slow arc, arrives at a gentle life.

Harmony stills. I close down
a quarry of soft causes forever.
Park now at a roadside shrine,
imagine the rented lives.

Remember our colour cures?
Polish your mirrors. And your lies.
Start up the second readings,
will you, in that glorious mansion voice?

We never cease to dream
of novel transgressions, and peace.
Light through rotted floors. Red
and white stories, waylaid by night.
We mask our parting woes. Compassion

a last condition. No trajectory of promises
extended in beads of desire. Gutted beliefs
thrash among splendour.

A faint scheme and an eye
for eye imbroglio. All or nothing
knife line of vision. A planned vista.
Keep your life and natural truth.
Who brandishes the finer stick?
It's a melt into coy country,
or an auction in the underworld.
We sit for avarice class, abandon
all claims on restitution. Harvest
failure from the blasted spines
of crippled planets – yes, they have us.

Drowning Pond

I live by a trail the storybook mind
made flesh; persist through tightening
blood vessels; plumb the character
of days. Circulate poisonously. Feel
only awe at the sweep and groaning
strength of troubling personalities.
Assess my bonds in triple book
fashion. Layers of illusion. Beauticians.
Dishevelled Phoenicians.
No economy of scale in nightmares
trotted out in razor-clear sunshine.

Watchtower

You learn the little mercies
seeing time unroll out here
in lassitude. A dead soul's
no impediment to building heat.
We run with the winds. Our appetite
for destruction grows. We know how
to handle a full circle of fretting
gods, even as more settlers arrive.
We fear only lightning and the febrile
crowd, track only our torpid metabolisms
among rough boulders,
graves, and endless patience.

Best Instincts

The cool garden fills with reptiles.
Hope's a damp thing that tends to break
over at times and send you in a spiral.
Seas harsher than necessary.
The warm heart battered, as usual.
We found the keys to the castle
and now our veins are clotted with new horrors.
We're figures loosed, uprooted, invincible, corrupted.
We inherit ravaged reasons to survive.

Blood Pressure

Idle and damned we grasp
the hands of the hopeless.
It's a cluttered view
from the bus. We are stricken
with doubt, beaten by absurdity,
measured by our endless statement.
The shadows are grainless children.
We build our bridges, target the temple,
master illusion in this place, with practice.
The screamers stay their abyss.
Mirrors remain behind closed doors,
the face of this horror purely
an object of metaphysical outreach.
We live our rock-solid security
beneath a glass battlefield (of course).

Tour of Duty

An old man down a dusty trail cares
no longer for durable constructions.
They've choked many wide worlds,
these immense hands
with their river-blue veins,
their sad measured intelligence.
We turn our backs and use our fingers,
climb foreign air, peel back the faces
of clouds, look for love outside time,
set aside our shiny tools, mend our ways.
No regret. Collect our sketches
from quiet rooms. Composed, we drown
in sincere intention. Our strong arms –
injected with hope – join bodies
migrating across the river into the steppe,
into a wash of superior purpose.
Full rebuilding of the cosmos
under way, shifting to that other dimension,
the one with pearls, anachronisms,
full threat and roar. Adoration, full threat.
Dream your tender universe, Friend,
and gauge your severe fragility.

Quietist Companion

It needed to be said so you chose exile
and moved even further from the known.
Where the leaves hang dead, consumed
by frost, rattling their poor rhythms,
ground suddenly firm, angled among monuments
of the cooled self, sharp, heavy, neatly
chaptered by the folded wings
of a faint moon gone missing.
The day in hallowed mood, brash
in mechanical flutter – all too fatal.

Night Ride

It's late and light's on its way
to some morose destination.
Let's live. Breathe. We're alone.
We're in love but the trail cools;
we walk away from the body,
our story shattered.

Animals graze there in postcard fields,
grass turning a bright ink. Our afternoons
in the doorways of fine citizens
at the end, entrails uneasy
against a background betraying
stark detail. Each fact floats away,
the dust of our world intact.

Rest in Time

A visit from sweet truth and ultimate love;
blood a minor miracle. Quest of light,
of idea. Perfection. Enter by the highway
winding into future valleys. In the arms
of the moment. All transient. Sinews and bonds.
A program. Catacomb and crowded world;
nature and her nest. Ambition.
It's over quickly, violently.
See her eyes now, amid a rash of angels.

Turning Home

We lie in the streetlight's faint plea
against the dark. Disband despite peace.
I turn home to your rich stories. Burn
an ear on your sumptuous peregrinations.
You were born into light, a hot quest
tempered by jagged lore. I'm aware of somnolent
legs, hope punching through ideology
and despair, heart held firm.

Far Light

We lost it all in a slow surrender;
we've nothing left but our sad numbers
aching in perfect still array. Empty
chairs and tables reveal the extent
of our majestic failures. We kissed
nihilism full on her full lips, listened
to the savage fog, for good grace,
passion, and the gallows. A sight
between black covers, inconsolable.

Harmony and Sea

You dealt me transposition, tempted me
with the blood of saviours; I can only
laugh and weep and wait for more death
in the morning mail, my country become
an empire choking beneath the weight
of its desire. Matters of time and recognition
both fade. We love our snakes and ceremonies,
love our blanched souls fleeing life.

Look North

Turning back through pain
and failing magic, falling back
I dream wide space and vague
ceremonies. No harmonies here
brushing whitened skin;
only cuts, a deep foray
to the bone, to the life
sentence parsed, swaggering
in a crowd, indomitable.

Acknowledgements

The poem, "New Rule," appeared in *Canadian Literature*. I deeply appreciate the support of the Ontario Arts Council. Particular thanks to John Donlan, Judith Fitzgerald, Ken Jalowica, Ronn Jefferies, and C. H. (Marty) Gervais.

Printed in June 2006
at Gauvin Press, Gatineau, Québec